A Question of Technology

Will robots take over the world?

and other questions about AI

Clive Gifford

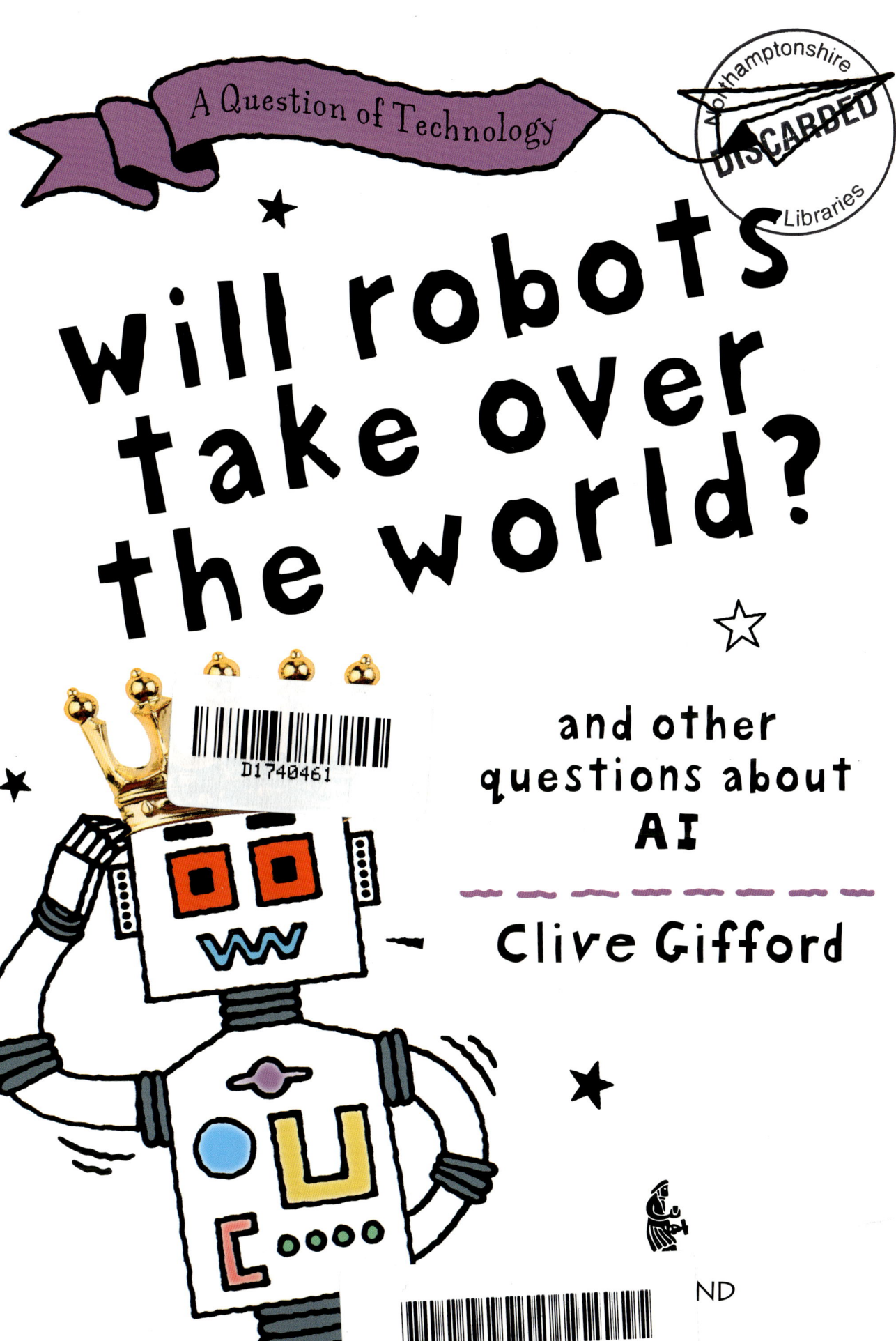

First published in Great Britain in 2023
by Wayland

© Hodder and Stoughton, 2023

Credits:
Editors: Julia Bird; Julia Adams
Design and illustrations: Matt Lilly
Cover design: Matt Lilly

HB ISBN 978 1 5263 2003 2
PB ISBN 978 1 5263 2002 5

Printed and bound in China

MIX
Paper from
responsible sources

FSC
www.fsc.org   FSC® C104740

Picture credits:

Alamy: Imagine China 29b; Rodrigo Reyes Marin/AFLO 25t.
© Ecorobotix SA: 11b.
ESA: 14t.
Getty Images: Blomberg 16b; Media News/Boston Herald 5tr; Ir
Schneider/LA Times 5tcl; SOPA Images/LightRocket 28b;
The Asahi Shimbun 12t; The Washington Post 5tcr;
Thamrongpat Theerathammakorn 8bl, 8cr; Ullstein Bild 6c.
JAXA: 15t.
NASA: Dryden/Carla Thomas 28t; Johnson Space Center 29t;
JPL-Caltech 14b.
NOAA: 24t.
Shutterstock: Michael Fitzsimmons 13b; Denis Klimov 18t;
Kateryna Kon 23b; Macondo front cover r, 1, 27b; New Africa 17t;
PastryShop 10t; Rozdemir 17c; Scharfsinn 11c; 24K Production
front cover l.
Waseda University Japan: 5tl.
Wikimedia Commons: Auscreative 23t CCA-SA-4 International;
A.Konby 6b PD.
Wyss Institute at Harvard University: 22b.

Every effort has been made to clear copyright.
Should there be any inadvertent omission, please
apply to the publisher for rectification.

Wayland
An imprint of
Hachette Children's Group
Part of Hodder and Stoughton
Carmelite House
50 Victoria Embankment
London EC4Y 0DZ

An Hachette UK Company
www.hachette.co.uk
www.hachettechildrens.co.uk

Contents

What is a robot?

Robots are fascinating, versatile machines designed to make our lives easier and safer. Robots can have many arms, or legs, or neither. They can be tall, short, squat or very long …

Key parts

While robots come in all shapes and sizes, most share some parts in common.

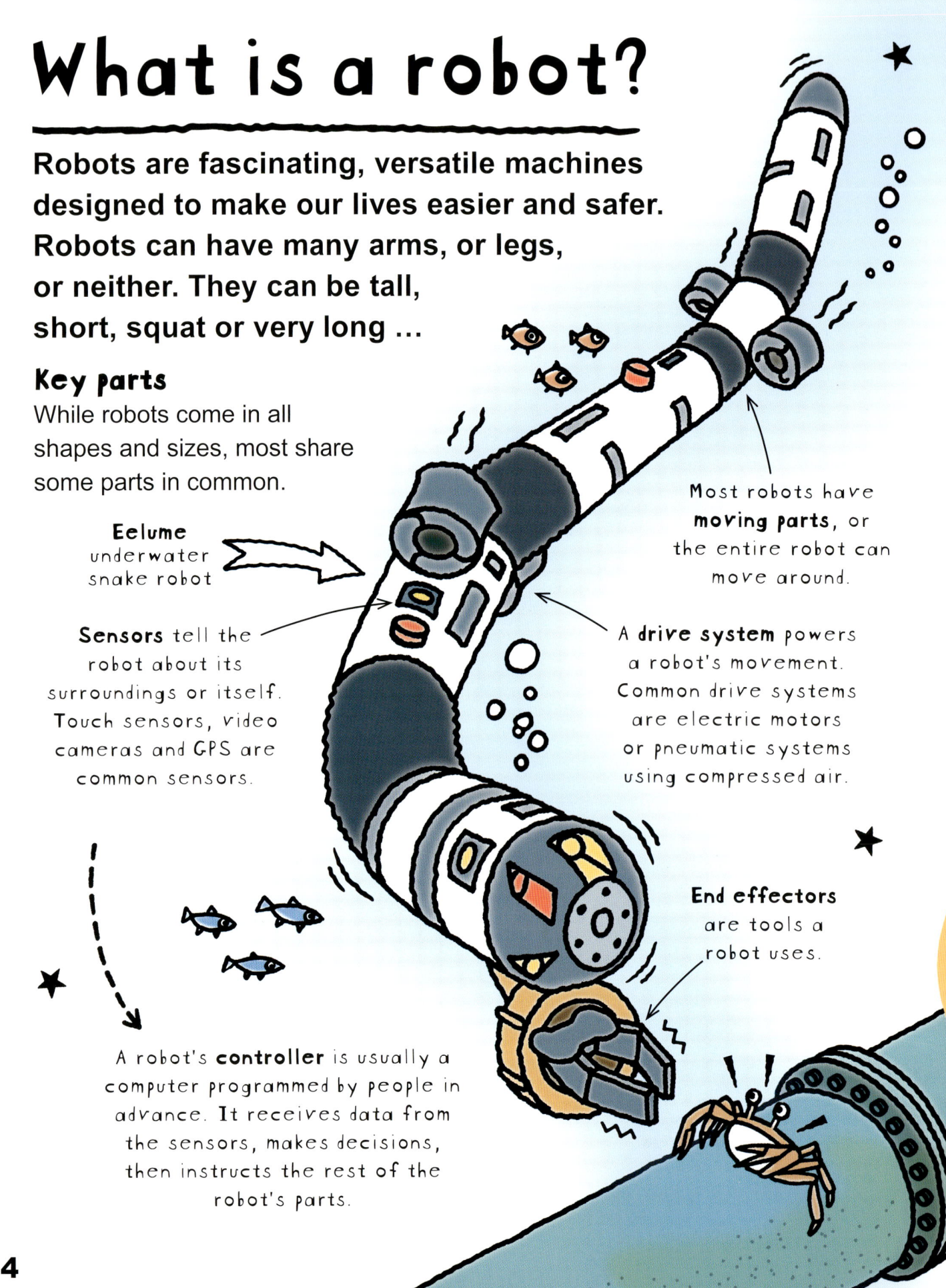

Eelume
underwater snake robot

Sensors tell the robot about its surroundings or itself. Touch sensors, video cameras and GPS are common sensors.

Most robots have **moving parts**, or the entire robot can move around.

A **drive system** powers a robot's movement. Common drive systems are electric motors or pneumatic systems using compressed air.

End effectors are tools a robot uses.

A robot's **controller** is usually a computer programmed by people in advance. It receives data from the sensors, makes decisions, then instructs the rest of the robot's parts.

4

Robotics pioneers

Some brilliant minds have helped turn robots from science fiction into science fact.

MY WAM-7R ROBOT COULD PLAY THE PIANO!

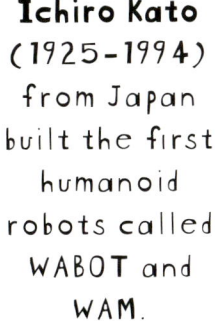

Ichiro Kato (1925-1994) from Japan built the first humanoid robots called WABOT and WAM.

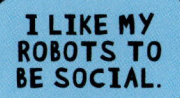

AN ASTEROID HAS BEEN NAMED AFTER ME!

US engineer **Donna Shirley** (1941-) was in charge of the team that built the Mars Sojourner robot – the first to move around another planet.

I LIKE MY ROBOTS TO BE SOCIAL.

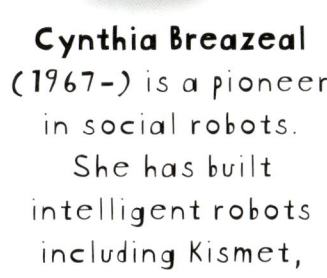

Cynthia Breazeal (1967-) is a pioneer in social robots. She has built intelligent robots including Kismet, Nexi and Jibo.

MY ROBOTS RUN!

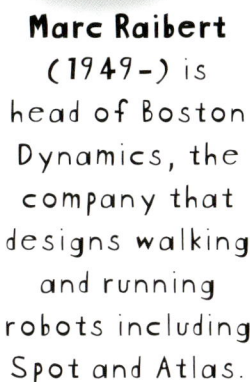

Marc Raibert (1949-) is head of Boston Dynamics, the company that designs walking and running robots including Spot and Atlas.

Robot workers

Robots are now found in all sorts of places, where they perform a wide range of jobs.

Floor cleaners

Space explorers

Receptionists

Fruit pickers

Metal welders

What was the first robot?

In 1961, a hefty one-and-a-half tonne robot arm began work in a car factory in the USA. Unimate #001 handled red-hot metal parts and was the first robot in a work setting.

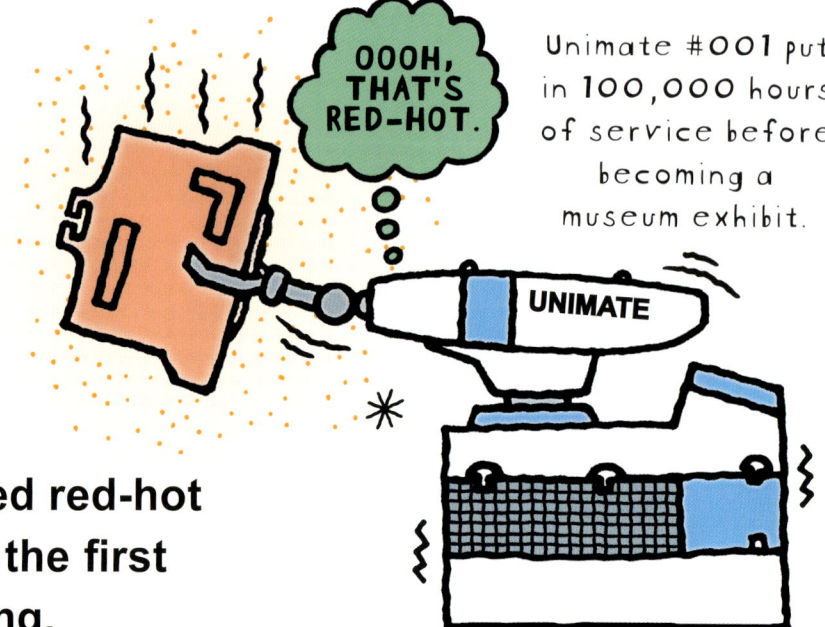

OOOH, THAT'S RED-HOT.

Unimate #001 put in 100,000 hours of service before becoming a museum exhibit.

UNIMATE

DEAR MUM ...

Model humans

Before Unimate, there were machines (automata) that looked like robots but didn't really make their own decisions, operate by themselves or perform a range of different jobs. Many were clockwork models of people, developed between the 17th and 19th centuries.

This automaton of a young boy actually handwrites short messages using a quill pen that it dips into a pot of ink.

Duck droid

French automata-maker Jacques de Vaucanson (1709–82) built a mechanical duck 280 years ago.

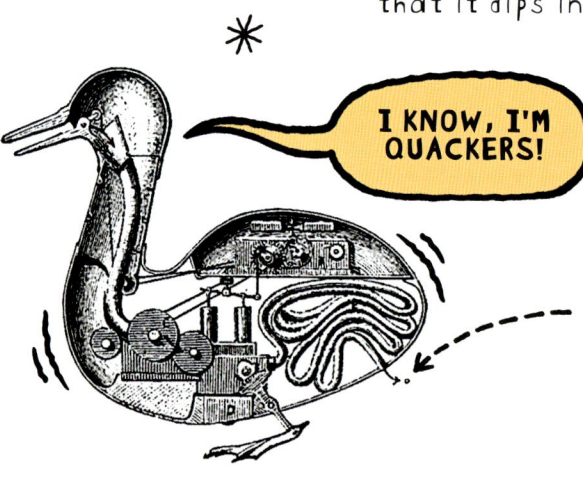

I KNOW, I'M QUACKERS!

The duck flapped its wings, ate seeds and pooped out droppings from its rear. Not the most useful device!

Electrifying exhibit

In the 1920s and 1930s, engineers built demonstration machines that used electricity to wow the public with seemingly amazing abilities.

Elektro, for example, was 2.1 m tall, could speak, blow up balloons and even answer questions …

Or so it seemed. The robot was in fact controlled by a person hidden away, connected by cables.

MY BRAIN IS BIGGER THAN YOURS!

Elektro

Real robots arrive

It wasn't until computing and electronics advanced in the 1960s and 1970s that real robots arrived to join Unimate #001.

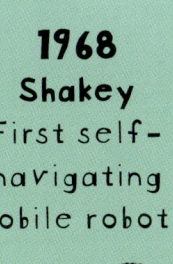

1968 Shakey
First self-navigating mobile robot.

1973 WABOT-1
Walked and used two cameras for eyes.

1974 T3
First robot arm controlled by a microcomputer.

How do robots know where to go?

Many robots are told where their final destination is, but have to find their own way there. This can involve hundreds of small but crucial actions and decisions.

Walk the line

One of the simplest systems sees colour coded lines painted on a factory or office floor. The robot uses two light sensors to stay positioned either side of the line.

FOLLOW THE YELLOW PAINT ROAD!

BEEP-BEEP-BEEP!

Thousands of robots called automated guided vehicles (AGVs) fetch and carry objects and materials around buildings using this system.

Bouncing back

Other robots use light sensors to detect obstacles on their route. They send out streams of infrared light waves that bounce off objects and return.

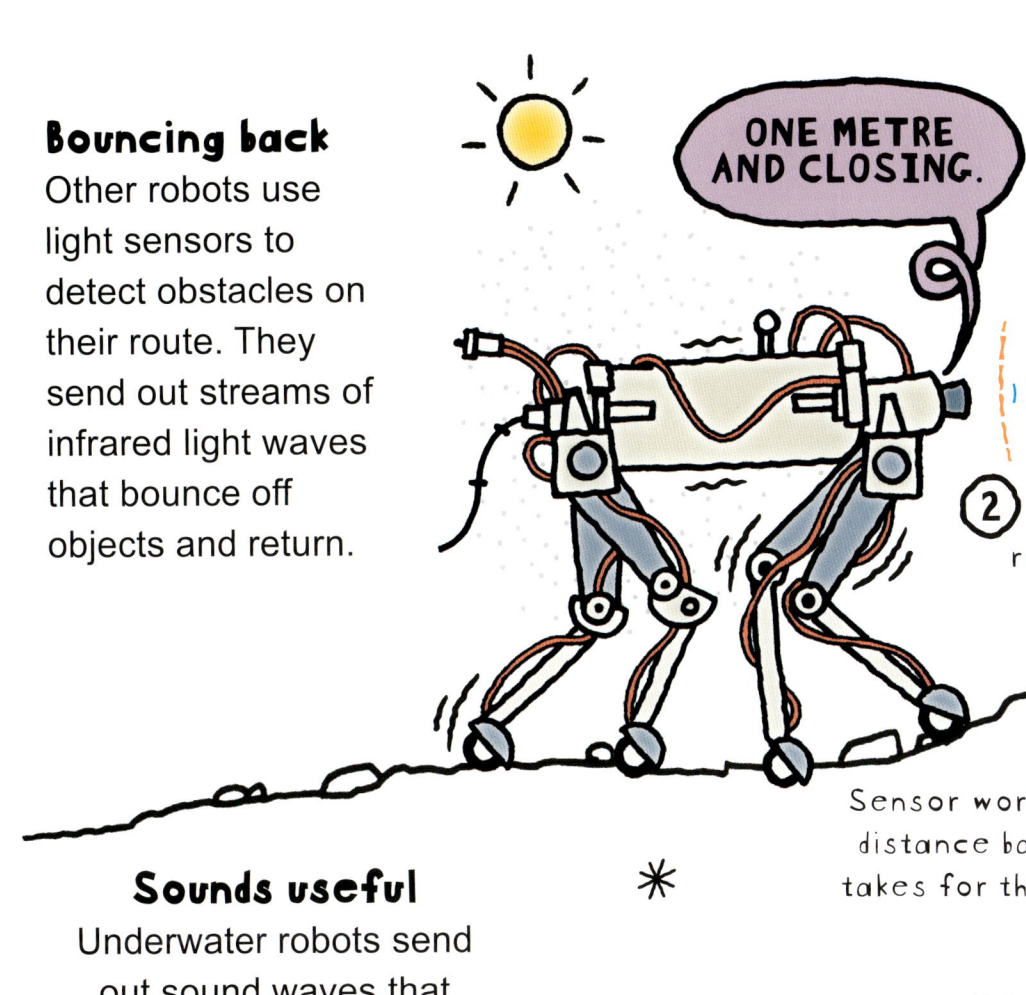

ONE METRE AND CLOSING.

① Sensor sends out light beam.

② Waves reflect off object.

③ Sensor works out the object's distance based on the time it takes for the waves to return.

Sounds useful

Underwater robots send out sound waves that also bounce off objects and return. These sonar systems allow robot subs to map the ocean floor and spot hazards.

Hazards ahead

Other sensors can also warn a robot of danger ahead. Tilt sensors can alert the robot when it is leaning so much it is in danger of tipping over, while temperature sensors can spot fires, lava or ice.

OOPS!

Why do robots get all the boring jobs?

It's true. Many robots do perform dull, repetitive tasks like sorting through rubbish all the time or picking and packing the same object 24/7.

The reason why robots get the boring jobs is simple.

They're so good at them!

Precision and repetition

Robots are super accurate. They can be programmed to perform the exact same task and move to precisely the same place within fractions of a millimetre.

Robots do not need toilet breaks breaks or lunch! Apart from the occasional repair, robots can work **ALL** the time.

Employee of the Month

J – bot IV

MORE WORK!

FEWER BREAKS!

Human v machine

While humans have other strengths, we just don't have the endurance and accuracy of robots. We can perform repetitive tasks for short periods, but longer sessions see our minds wander, our muscles ache and accuracy drop.

ZZZZZ!

I'M AWAKE 24/7.

Top jobs

Some robots do perfom more exciting jobs, however. They get to fight fires, defuse bombs or dive underwater to investigate new forms of sea life and old shipwrecks. A handful even get to head off into space to explore other worlds!

Robo-farms

Robots are becoming important in farms as well as factories.

I WISH THEY'D LET ME PICK ORANGES FOR A CHANGE!

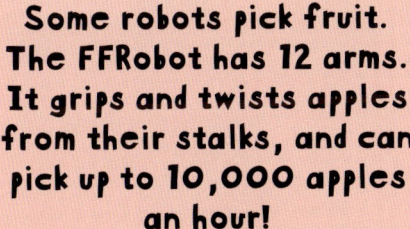

Some robots pick fruit. The FFRobot has 12 arms. It grips and twists apples from their stalks, and can pick up to 10,000 apples an hour!

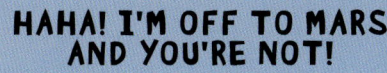

An Ecorobotix robot can detect and remove weeds from up to three hectares of farm fields a day. That's about the size of 119 tennis courts.

HAHA! I'M OFF TO MARS AND YOU'RE NOT!

How do robots save lives?

In lots of ways. Sometimes they come directly to the rescue. At other times, they warn of hazards, prevent disasters or provide medical assistance.

ROBEAR lifts patients in and out of beds and wheelchairs.

Lifesaver!

In 2018, the Little Ripper flying robot started work as a lifeguard at Lennox Heads, Australia. Its main job was to spot sharks in the waters below using a powerful camera.

THANKS LITTLE RIPPER!

On its first day at work, it helped rescue two swimmers in trouble. Little Ripper dropped a flotation device that they clung to until human lifeguards could reach them. **Hero!**

WHERE THERE'S RUBBLE, THERE'S OFTEN TROUBLE!

Snakebots

When disaster strikes, some robots hunt for survivors. Snakebots can bend their bodies and worm their way between gaps in rubble. They use microphones to hear and thermal imagers to detect heat given off by survivors.

Other snakebots are equipped with sensors that can detect gas and chemical pipe leaks so that they can be fixed BEFORE they cause a disaster.

HMMM. THAT SMELLS... DISASTROUS.

NICE BAG BUT NOT MY COLOUR.

Explosive events

Hundreds of robots work detecting and disarming bombs and other hazardous packages. Controlled by experts from a safe distance, these robots approach suspicious packages, film them and use sensors to analyse any chemicals they contain.

Radio antenna sends data and receives commands in return.

Multiple cameras send back images to human bomb disposal staff.

Robot grippers can lift and open packages or move them away from danger.

Tracks like a tank allow robot to climb up and down steps.

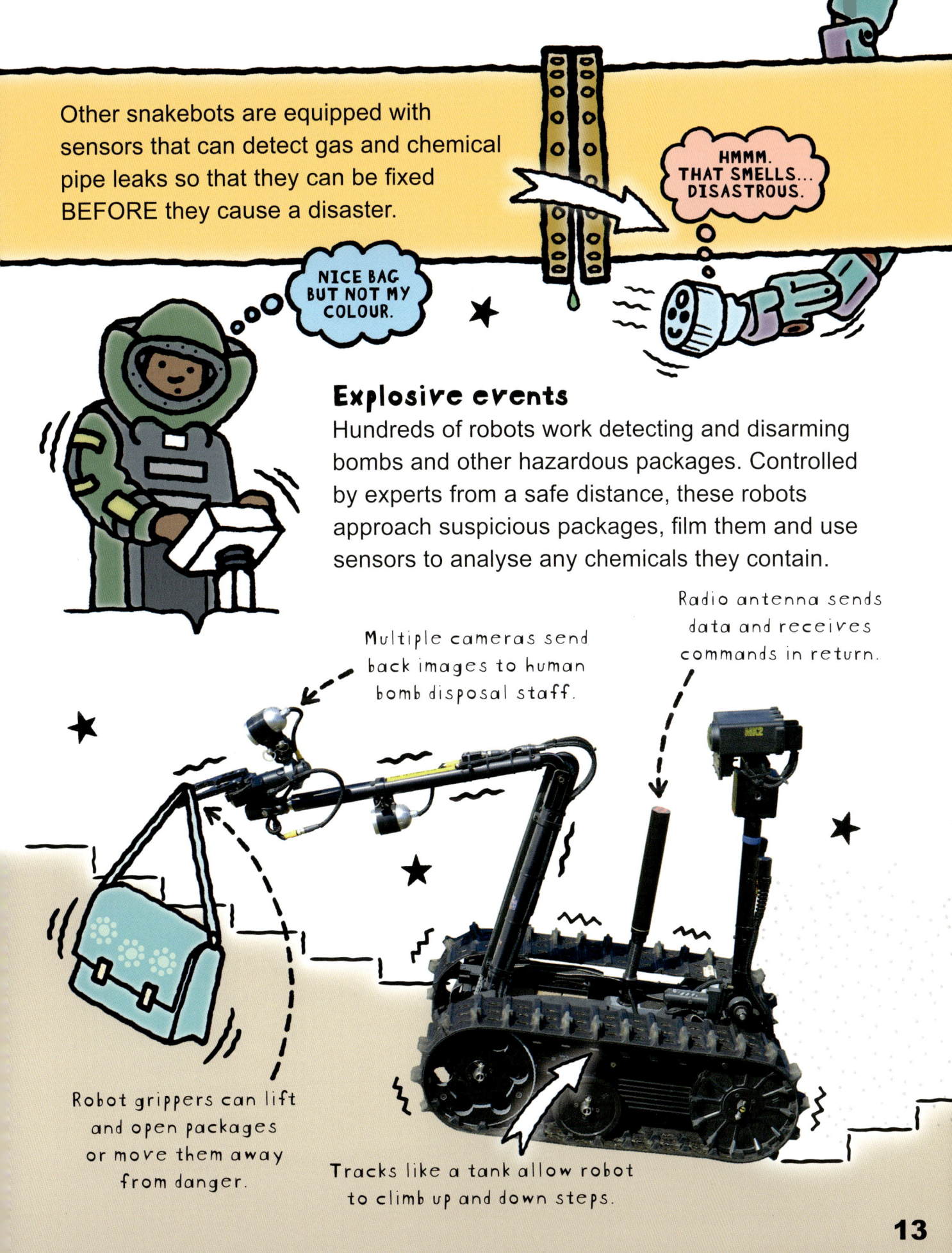

Why are some robots astronauts?

Putting robots in space seems like a lot of work. And space robots are VERY expensive. But they do offer many advantages over people.

Robots can be built tough and resistant to radiation, extreme heat and cold and other threats in space. Humans have only travelled in space as far as the Moon. Robots, though, can voyage much further.

ROBOTS 1 HUMANS 0

I COST US$100 MILLION AND AM WORTH EVERY PENNY!

Philae landed on a comet in 2014.

ROBOTS 2 HUMANS 0

Tireless effort

Now, even if we could send people to many of these places, would they do a better job there than robots?

The Curiosity rover on Mars, for example, has taken over 800,000 photos and worked solidly for 10 years without a break. As a human, that's impossible to beat!

NO NEED FOR NAPS!

Weighty questions

The lighter a space mission, the easier it is to launch. This is another advantage for robots over humans.

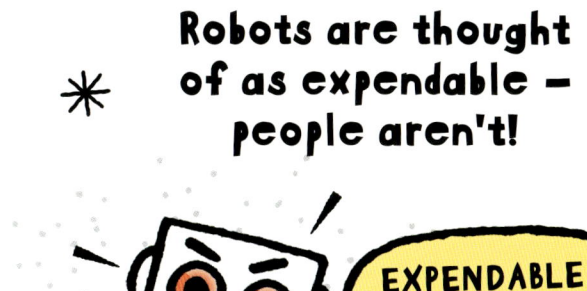

 This is HIBOU, which landed on an asteroid in 2018.

While each person may weigh a lot less than a hefty robot like the 1,000-kg Perseverance Mars rover, human astronauts travel with a lot of luggage. They need all their food, water, air and medical supplies, along with places to eat, sleep and work, (and not forgetting a toilet). This all adds up to tonnes of weight.

By contrast, robots need little more than a power supply. They can also be sent on one-way trips – far easier to organise and cheaper than challenging return missions.

I'M ONLY GOING FOR A WEEK!

Robots are thought of as expendable – people aren't!

EXPENDABLE... ME?

Will robots take all our jobs?

By the time you leave school, college or university, there will definitely be more robots around. But will those pesky bots have taken all the jobs?

ARE YOU POWERED BY ELECTRIC MOTORS TOO?

Bot boom

As robots get more powerful and flexible, their numbers in industry are **BOOMING**. Some smart factories now contain more robots than people!

Thousands of robots have jobs in warehouses, ferrying, stacking and packing parcels for delivery to online shoppers. Some are even delivering packages direct.

Other robots work in places that humans couldn't or wouldn't want to, such as inspecting sewage and chemicals pipes from the inside, and cleaning homes.

FIRST BOT THERE GETS AN OIL BATH!

STINKY!

THIS JOB REALLY SUCKS!

The most common home robots are vacuum cleaners. There were just hundreds of these 20 years ago. Today, there are more than 25 million!

New roles

But robots won't steal **ALL** the jobs. They'll also help create many new ones, especially in fields such as coding, analysing data and engineering.

A person guides a robot through all parts of its new task.

Thomas Edison, 1847-1931, helped invent the record player, movie camera and the light bulb.

No worries

Robots are great at some tasks, but not so good at many others – including creative thinking, problem-solving and dealing directly with people.

Nor do they make great writers, vets, physiotherapists or inventors. Jobs in these and many other areas are likely to be safe for a long time to come.

PHEW!

Why don't more robots look like us?

Robots in early sci-fi shows were mostly human-shaped as it was easier for actors and costume makers! This gave the impression that humanoid robots would be common in the future.

Fast-forward 50 or 60 years and only a handful of humanoids are at work. Most that do exist are used for research or demonstrations.

It turns out that a human shape is great for us, but not quite so good for moving machines.

The key reason is balance.

ASIMO can climb stairs — a rare skill for a robot.

Balancing act

Being a human is a constant balancing act. Most humans are tall and have two legs.

You also rest on relatively small feet for your height. **WELL DONE!**

When you move, you lift one leg off the ground and actually balance on just the one foot.

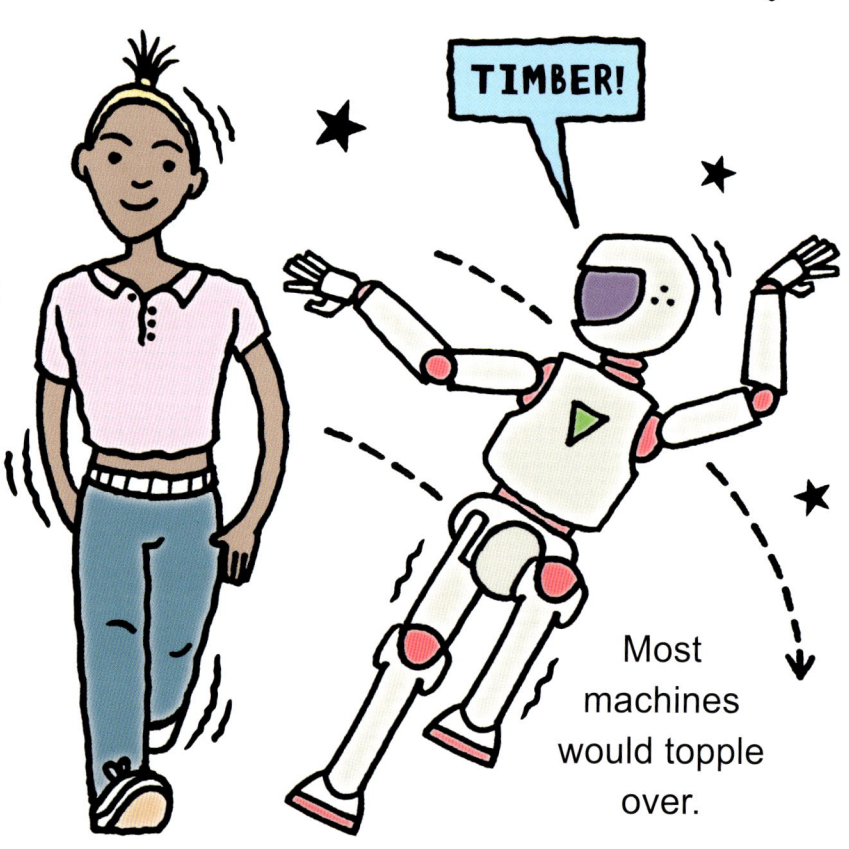

TIMBER!

Most machines would topple over.

You, however, possess three things:

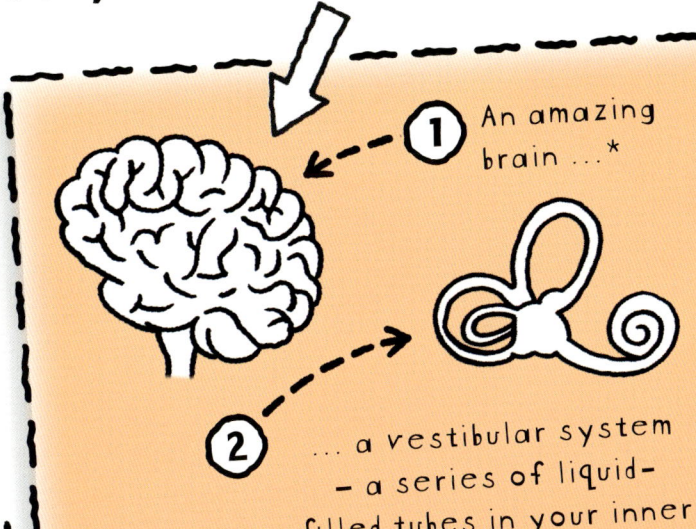

1. An amazing brain ...*

2. ... a vestibular system – a series of liquid-filled tubes in your inner ear that constantly measure your position and balance ...

3. ... and more than 600 muscles around your body.

Acting on data from your vestibular system, your brain commands your muscles and joints to make small adjustments to keep you balanced.

It's an incredible system that mobile robots struggle to match. This is why other body shapes and ways of moving are often chosen by robot designers.

* Not to scale.

Wheely nice

Many mobile robots move on wheels or tracks like a bulldozer.

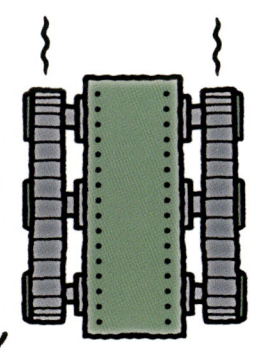

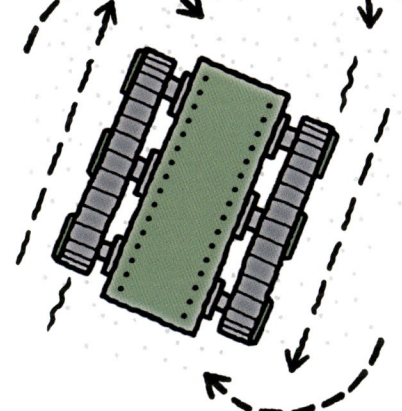

Most of them turn by reversing one of their tracks so the robot skids round.

Insect success

Some robots are modelled on insects. They stay balanced by keeping three feet on the ground as they lift and move the other three.

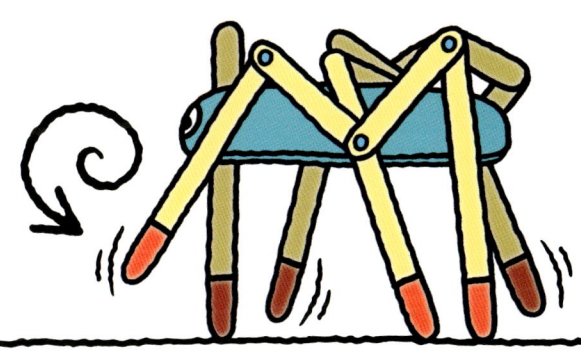

Three legs form a stable triangular base.

Does a robot know it's holding an orange?

When a robot grabs hold of a banana, an orange or some other fruit, does it actually know what it's getting to grips with?

Well, yes and no. Unlike us, robots don't know much about oranges but they can be programmed to spot one using their sensors.

Some robots use cameras to scan a scene in front of them and separate out all the objects they view.

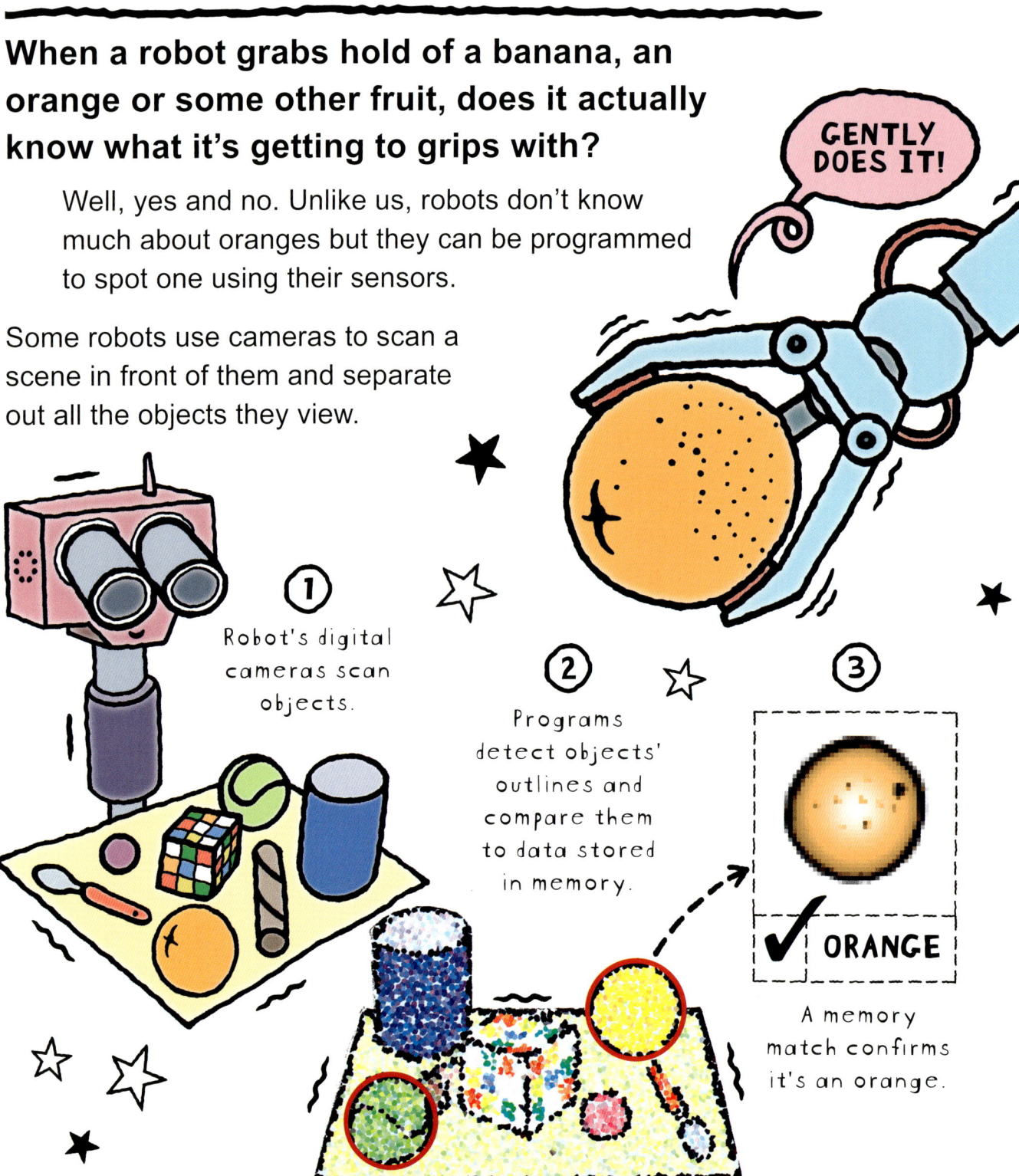

GENTLY DOES IT!

① Robot's digital cameras scan objects.

② Programs detect objects' outlines and compare them to data stored in memory.

③ A memory match confirms it's an orange.

✓ ORANGE

Gripping stuff

Identifying an object is just the start. A robot needs further instructions to follow, such as which part of the object is best to grip and how much force it should use.

OOPS, TOO MUCH!

Touch sensor tells robot how much of the gripper is in contact with the object.

Actuators in hand adjust amount of force each finger presses with.

Signals from controller tell hand to exert more or less force.

Is seeing believing?

Now, matching outlines, shapes and colours to ones held in memory is not *quite* the same process as seeing is for us. Our powerful brain processes views from our eyes and sometimes fills in gaps by using its other knowledge and making assumptions.

Many robots are not so good at filling in. But even your brain is not 100 per cent foolproof.

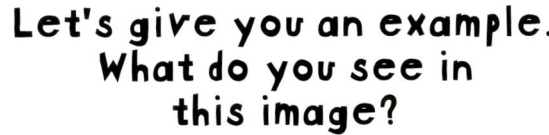

Let's give you an example. What do you see in this image?

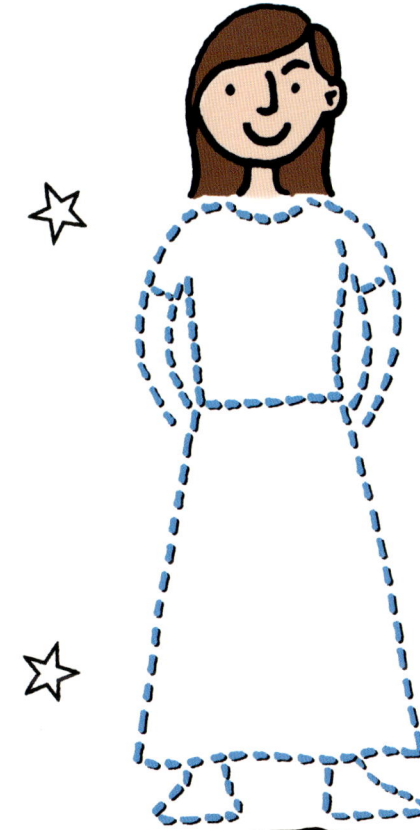

Nine out of ten people see an orange triangle sitting on top of three black circles. They're wrong! There's no triangle, just three partial circles, but your brain reckons it knows best and has filled in the gaps …

INCORRECTLY!

How small can robots go?

Robots started out big and chunky because computers, power sources and electronics were all big, too. As these have sh_{runk} in size but gr**OWN** in power, robots can be built smaller.

Why build tiny?

Small robots can work in areas and perform tasks that larger machines cannot. Being lighter means they need less power to move. Some are cheaper to build than big bots and can be replaced more easily if damaged.

Actual size

RoBeetle crawls on four legs and weighs just 0.09g – about the same as three grains of rice.

Tiny fliers

Micro aerial vehicles are small flying robots. They're useful for flying unnoticed (good for spying and filming wildlife) or in restricted space such as between trees or in disaster areas.

The smallest flying robot so far is RoboBee. It weighs just 0.08g, sits on a fingertip and flaps its wings 120 times a second.

Robot swarms

Large numbers of small robots may one day work together. Robot swarms could scour the countryside or seas, checking on crops or wildlife, for example.

DAVE ... DAVE! ANYONE SEEN DAVE?

The biggest working swarm so far contains 1,024 Kilobots. These 3.3-cm-tall research robots communicate with each other using infrared signals. They can flock together or move to form different patterns.

Will robots get even smaller?

Some engineers certainly think so. They're trying to build nano-robots – machines measured in nanometres. One nanometre = 0.000001 mm. That's very small.

Hundreds of nano-robots could occupy the space taken by the full stop at the end of this sentence. And they could prove incredibly useful in tackling pollution or repairing machines.

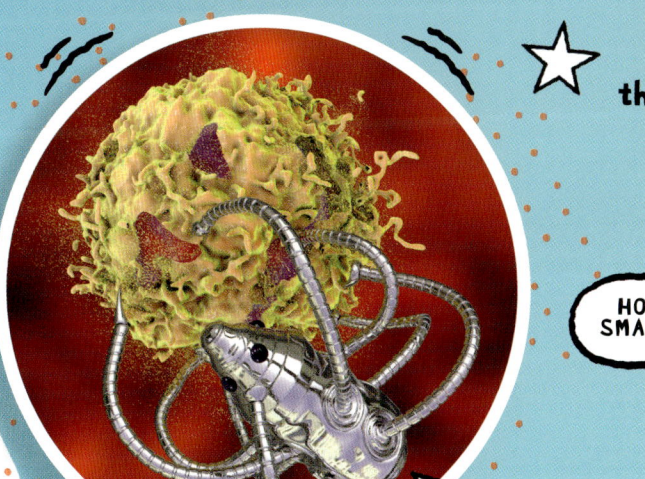

GOTCHA!

HOW SMALL?

ON AVERAGE, A HUMAN HAIR IS 80,000 NANOMETRES WIDE!

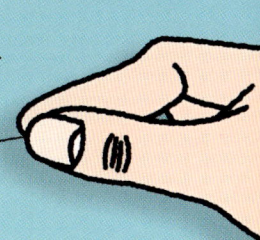

They may even be capable of repairing people. **Amazing!**

A future nano-robot, injected into a person, could find and destroy a harmful cell.

Can robots save the planet?

Possibly. Although robots use up materials when made and need electricity to run, some are starting to pay the planet back. How? By tackling pollution and climate change and re-greening the planet.

Powered by waves and sunlight, Wave Gliders cruise the oceans sending back water pollution measurements by radio.

Rubbish robots

Waste is a growing problem. Sorting through litter is dirty, dangerous work, so robots are starting to do the job. Some can pick through 32,000 items a day, sending many objects for recycling.

Robot's cameras detect common objects such as plastic bottles.

Rubbish robots, such as SeaVax and WasteShark are looking to clean up rivers and oceans by scooping up harmful waste in the water. Other robotic boats may cruise the seas, cleaning up oil slicks and other water pollution.

One WasteShark robot can collect up to 500 kg of rubbish a day.

Power up

People will rely more on solar panels and wind turbines to generate electricity in the future. Robots could help monitor and repair these devices so they produce as much clean electricity as possible.

Removing dust can lead to solar panels creating 25 per cent more electricity.
Brilliant!

I'M RE-GREENING THE PLANET!

Going green

Planting more trees helps to re-wild previously damaged land and can help tackle climate change. Robots that can work by themselves and plant tree seedlings could help to build new forests.

THANK YOU, ECO-BOTS!

If all these, as well as other eco-bots, were deployed in large numbers, they might make a **HUGE** difference.

Will robots take over the world?

You've probably read stories or watched movies about robots taking over the planet. Is there any truth in them?

What's in a word?

The word 'robot' was first used in the 1920 play "R.U.R." by a Czech writer Karel Čapek. He took it from the Czech word *robota*, meaning forced work or drudgery. His play saw robots rise up, rebel and conquer people.

DROIDS R US!

DROIDS AGAINST DRUDGERY

ROBOT RIGHTS!

Sensors gather data

Programs analyse data

Controller makes decisions

Robots' parts perform actions

Under control

In reality, a robot rebellion would be tricky, simply because of how robots work. They rely on their controller to make decisions. But the controller is only as smart and capable as the programs it runs, which are all written by people.

Feedback and failsafes

Robots that work near or with people have safety features built in. These often include a manual override which allows people to take control and stop the robot instantly.

ZZZZZZZ!

ON
CLICK!
OFF

Many robot controllers and the programs they run have failsafes built in. These are often computer code that cuts power or shuts it down should the robot malfunction in any way.

Machine learning

Robots are being developed that are able to learn about objects and actions for themselves, rather than just follow programs. In the future, these may be much smarter than today's bots, but will still follow rules and have failsafes and other safety features.

DON'T WORRY, I JUST LIKE DRESSING UP!

So, could it happen in the future?
Relax.
It's very, very unlikely that future robots could break their programming, become supreme leaders over all beings and make us their slaves.

HONEST!

27

Quick-fire questions

Global Hawk robot

872

CRIKEY, NO PILOT!

What's the farthest a robot has travelled?

The winners are space robots that have travelled millions of kilometres through the solar system. On Earth, a Global Hawk robot aircraft flew itself from the USA to Australia in 2001, covering a distance of 13,840 km. A Wave Glider robot (see page 24) pipped it in 2012, travelling 14,703 km.

Do robots have feelings?

No, not real ones. Robots can sense their surroundings and themselves. Some can report if their parts aren't working or their batteries need recharging, but they don't have emotions. However, some robots can appear emotional. They can move their head parts or use a screen as a face and change their expression to show joy, surprise or unhappiness.

AM I REAL?

What's the most a robot can lift?

The FANUC M-2000iA/2300 robot arm is the current heavyweight world champion. It can lift 2,300 kg, meaning it can pick up an entire car with ease. Out in space where there is next-to-no gravity, the Canadarm2 robot arm can lift even more. It is attached to the International Space Station and handles spacecraft with a mass of up to 116,000 kg.

Will robots win the football World Cup?

Robots *do* play football and even have their own international competition, called RoboCup. Taking part against or alongside humans is a long way off, though!

BEATS ONE, GOES ROUND ANOTHER ...

Glossary

Actuator A device like an electric motor that moves a part of a robot.

Antenna A device, usually a long slender aerial, which helps send and receive wireless signals using radio waves.

Assembly line A line of machines and workers in a factory along which a product moves as it is constructed.

Atmosphere The blanket of gases that surround a planet.

Automaton A mechanical figure designed to produce a lifelike series of actions.

Autonomous A machine that makes decisions and works by itself.

Controller The part of the robot that makes decisions and tells the other parts of the robot what to do. It is usually a computer.

Database An organised collection of information that allows data to be easily searched and retrieved.

Drone A pilot-less flying machine, usually remote-controlled by a person on the ground.

Evaporate To turn from liquid into a vapour or gas.

Expendable Not so important so seen as okay if it is lost or destroyed.

Failsafe Either hardware or computer code that automatically stops a robot running if there is a problem.

Feedback Useful information about a situation or how a task is going, sent back to the robot by its sensors.

Global Positioning System (GPS) A navigation system using a series of satellites orbiting Earth to give an accurate position on Earth.

Humanoid A robot that looks a lot like a partial or complete person and performs human-like actions.

Hydraulics A power system using liquids in cylinders found in some robots.

Infrared A type of electromagnetic radiation, like light, but not visible to our eyes.

Machine learning The ability of a robot or other device to gain knowledge from the information it collects, rather than solely through being programmed by people.

Manual override A control that allows a person to take charge and suspend the actions of an automatic machine like a robot.

Nanometre A microscopic unit of distance. One nanometre is equal to a billionth of a metre. An average human hair has a width of 80-100,000 nanometres.

Nanotechnology The science of building machines and robots at a scale of nanometres.

Pneumatics A way of powering moving parts of a robot using compressed air or other gases.

Program The series of instructions given to a robot or computer. When run, they enable the machine to perform a task.

Prototype A first version of a device made to test it or to raise publicity.

Sensor A device that collects information about a robot or its surroundings.

Thermal imager A device that detects infrared radiation given off by warm objects or beings.

Welding A way of joining together two pieces of metal or certain types of plastic using heat.

Further reading

Websites

www.youtube.com/watch?v=6L-V4xzUcmM
See robots that can lift cars, recycle rubbish and other tasks
in this top 10 industrial robots video.

https://kidscodecs.com/what-is-artificial-intelligence
Read this long, brilliant article and you'll understand a lot more
about artificial intelligence and how it works with robots.

https://robots.ieee.org
This excellent website is packed with photos and features
about dozens of amazing robots, sorted into different types.

www.youtube.com/watch?v=KTpRiPFbmuE
See how the iCub humanoid robot learns
about objects and compares them to others in this BBC video.

https://mars.nasa.gov/mars2020/
Get the latest news on the Perseverance rover currently exploring Mars.

Books

A Robot World
by Clive Gifford (Franklin Watts, 2019)

The Tech-Head Guide: AI
by William Potter (Wayland, 2021)

Explore AI: Intelligent Robots
by Sonya Newland (Wayland, 2022)

Robots: Meet The Machines Of The Future
(DK, 2018)

How to Design the World's Best Robot
by Paul Mason (Wayland, 2018)

Index